Reading
Stock Charts

A Beginner's Guide
to
Technical Analysis

The One Hour Expert Series

Heather Cullen

Copyright © 2023
Heather Cullen

Disclaimer

The ideas and strategies in this book are simply describing what has worked — and what hasn't worked - for me. The information in this book is for educational purposes only and is not investment advice. I am not a financial advisor or investment adviser and advise that you consult a licensed financial advisor to determine the suitability of any investment.

While I have spent many hours checking and rechecking the figures in the book, I make no representation as to the accuracy or completeness of the information and will not be liable for any errors or omissions. The author assumes no responsibility or liability for trading and investment results, losses, injuries, or damages. It should not be assumed that the ITM strategies will be profitable and will not result in losses. It is not a replacement for professional financial and investment advice.

Dedication

To
Ben & Elise,
Willow & Flynn

This is a 'Short Read'

After writing four full-sized books, and having lots of questions and comments from readers, I realized that sometimes people just want to know about a particular stock market topic without having to wade through an entire book, much of which they already know.

Sometimes people just need a refresher on a specific subject but can't remember exactly where they read it, so they have to delve through several books to find it.

To address this need, I decided to write a series of short books on individual topics in the stock market. I selected the twelve topics based on what elicited the most questions from readers. This book, Reading Stock Charts, is the third 'short read' to be published and is part of the One Hour Expert stock market series.

The information covered in these books is too much for a simple report, but the scope is too limited for a full-sized book. It's more like a short story rather than a novel or a newspaper article. These books are designed to be read in an hour or so. I know everyone has a busy life!

Contents

HeatherCullen.com

Introduction

Being able to read stock charts is essential for the successful trader. Trying to navigate the market without this basic tool is setting yourself up for failure which, naturally, we don't want! Technical indicators are there to help us make sense of these charts, and to let us see what is really going on. That being said, there are a lot of wild claims about the accuracy and efficacy of indicators on stock charts.

**No indicator works all of the time;
most indicators work some of the time.**

With hindsight, it is easy to pick out situations where they worked and show that as 'proof' of how effective they are; there are any number of books that do that. What is not normally shown in books are situations where they didn't work. In this book, I have tried to show both sides of the story, situations where they worked and situations where they didn't.

There are hundreds of indicators, and no single book could hope to cover them all; instead, I have picked the top indicators, the one most used by traders. We separate the ones that are entirely dependent on the user drawing them correctly and those that are mathematically computed. These objective indicators are not totally free of human bias; they are also subject to human interpretation.

Of course, traders can go over the top; I've seen charts with so many indicators that it is hard to even identify the actual prices far less work out what the price action was doing. Simplicity is the key. The price action, as shown by the candlesticks, is the real data; the indicators are what we use to interpret this data. Knowing what we are looking for and then selecting the right indicators to enable us to see it is where the skill lies.

It is important to keep a clear head when reading charts, and resist the temptation to see what you would like to see rather than what is actually there. Your success as a trader depends on you doing this, and not getting caught up in a narrative which the facts don't support.

The stock market is like the ocean; it has waves, and it has tides. To be successful you have to trade with the tide and not be distracted by the waves. Indicators help you by removing the day to day 'noise' of the waves and let you focus on the tide. That is where success in the stock market lies.

Trade the tide, not the waves.

Technical analysis works precisely because people look at it. And if people care, I care.

John Bollinger

Ch 1. Traders & Candlesticks

Understanding the stock market starts with being able to read stock charts. Essentially, stock charts are simple representations of historical price movements which enable traders to see the past performance of a stock and trends. They show what the prices were on particular dates, whether it is trending up or down, and how many traders were buying and selling the stock.

So far so good; this is objective data, and everyone looking at a stock chart sees exactly the same chart. But traders may **'see'** different things.

Traders interpret what is on the chart, then use their interpretation for their decision-making. They decide, based on their interpretation, whether a stock is likely to go up (and they will buy) or down (and they will sell). These different interpretations can make reading stock chart reading seem like an arcane artform.

Optical Illusions

As for works of art, people look at stock charts and see them from their own perspective, and like works of art, people can see different things. Take this classic example of an optical illusion is it a duck or a rabbit? Most people are able to see both, and can switch between seeing the rabbit and the duck, but both are an interpretation. Whether we see the rabbit or the duck that is an interpretation; that we are actually seeing is an arrangement of lines on a page.

Why is it important to understand that chart reading can depend on the person reading it? Because when we are reading a stock chart it is important to see what is actually there, rather than what we think is there. Context, expectation and past experiences all shape our perceptions. For example, in the above illusion, at Easter, when chocolate bunnies are everywhere, people are more likely to see the rabbit than the duck.

Our brain specializes in making quick assumptions and making sense of things, and so fills in what it considers 'missing' information. Unfortunately, when many people look at stock charts, they see what they expect to see (or, often, what they want to see) rather than what is actually there.

This can reach absurd heights, for example in Elliott Wave Theory where stocks are supposed to move in fractal patterns (yes, really!), but no two practitioners can agree on where exactly the waves start and end. I traded using Elliott Wave theory some years ago, I can attest that (a) I lost money and (b) it is only possible to 'identify' the waves after the entire pattern had completed, which is not very helpful!

Stock charts themselves are completely objective; anyone being given the same data would make exactly the same stock chart, but people then interpret what is on the chart, introducing subjectivity.

Interpreting Stock Charts

To understand the market and to understand what goes on in traders' minds, we have to know what they are looking at, what they are 'seeing' and the actions they are likely to then take.

To interpret stock charts, traders use **technical indicators,** and analyzing stock charts with indicators is called **technical analysis.** Traders who base their trading decisions on technical analysis are often called **chartists**.

This is opposed to being a **fundamentals** trader. Fundamental traders base their decisions on information about the stock itself, like the balance sheet, assets and cash flow statements rather than the stock chart.

Technical indicators can be **objective indicators**, that are calculated mathematically (like a moving average or Bollinger Bands) or they can be **subjective indicators** (like head-and-shoulders patterns, or Elliott Wave patterns) where the indicator relies on individual interpretation and trader discretion.

This book is about technical analysis, and will enable you to read stock charts, and importantly, to be able to distinguish between objective information and subjective information. So, let's start.

Japanese Candlesticks

Candlestick charts are relatively recent in the Western world, having been introduced in 1991, but they originated in Japan, sometime in the eighteenth or nineteenth century. Then, they were not applied to the stock market but used to record and analyze rice prices.

Nowadays, candlesticks are widely used to describe price movements of stocks, derivatives and currencies. Most stock charts use candlesticks because they give the information in an easy pictorial form.

You may already be familiar with candlestick charts but let's review what we know so that we are all starting with the same understanding. If we want to summarize what a stock did on any day, then there are four measures that are important:

> The open price

> The close price

> The highest price

> The lowest price

There is a fifth measure that is important: the volume of sales, but that is not included in the candlestick chart, but displayed on a separate graph, usually underneath the main graph.

A candlestick is a way of capturing the open / high / low / close graphically. Below are 2 typical candlesticks, one an UP day, the other a DOWN day, and you can see that they capture all the above.

Candlesticks have a body and two shadows (or wicks). The colored box is called the body of the candle, and the lines at the top and the bottom are called the shadows.

The body is made from the open and close prices, the tip of the top shadow is the high of the day, and the tip of the bottom shadow the low. The size of the body and shadows vary widely, depending on the trades that happened that day.

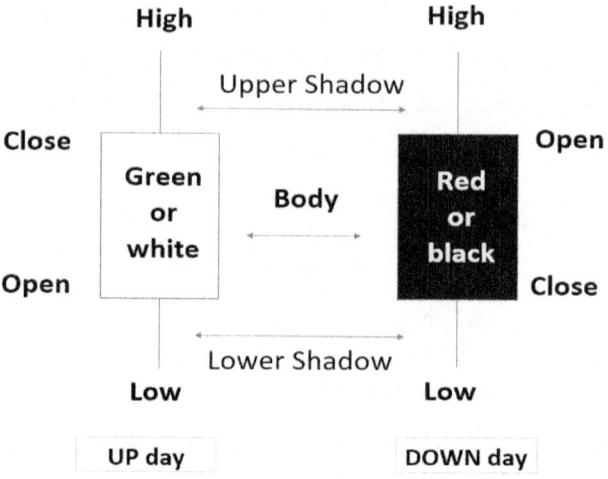

> ➤ Candlesticks are usually colored green if the close price is higher than the open price (an UP day) or white if no color is possible. (as in this book!)

> ➤ Candlesticks are usually colored red if the close price is lower than the open price (a DOWN day) and black if no color is possible.

Candlestick Charts

Usually, traders look at daily charts, but the chart be for any time period you choose. It can be a week, a month, a quarter or a year. It can be hourly, or every 15 minutes or every minute. The same candlesticks are used no matter what time period you are using.

Traders choose the time period that suits their way of trading, and in our case, it is the daily chart.

Day traders (or, as I think they are more appropriately termed, 'temporary traders') will use 5-minute or 1-minute charts. Long term investors may only look at weekly or monthly charts. I suggest that you look at the daily charts and occasionally look at the weekly chart just to check that you have the bigger picture.

If you have read any of my other books you will know that I use an analogy of the ocean for the stock market, and recommend you trade the tide not the waves. In stock charts the 5-minute and 1-minute charts show the waves. The daily and weekly charts tell you about the tide.

To see how a stock performs over time we can look at a candlestick chart. We read the date on the bottom axis and the price on the side axis. On most charts you have the option of changing your cursor to 'crosshairs' which makes reading off the axes easier. Above is the chart for Google (Alphabet) in 2020 showing the big dip because of the coronavirus, and then its subsequent recovery. The prices are on the right and the date on the bottom.

Types of Candlesticks

Candlesticks can look wildly different. The body can be short or long, or even just a horizontal line, which would mean that the open and close price was the same. The shadows may be short or long, there may be only one shadow, or there may be no shadows at all.

The different types of candlesticks describe the actions of traders and the mood of the market. Individual candle types can have names, and combinations of candles, or patterns, have names and have different meanings. However, all are a diagrammatical representation of traders' emotions during period you are looking at.

> ➢ Long body candles show there is a lot of buying (green / white) or selling (red / black) pressure.

> ➢ Short body candles show that there is very little price movement because traders

have no real conviction on the way the price is going.

➤ Short shadows show that most of the trading was near or between the open and close

➤ Long upper shadows show that buyers (bulls) dominated for a while, bidding the price up, but then the sellers (bears) forced the prices down.

➤ Long lower shadow show sellers (bears) dominated for a while, driving the price down, but then buyers (bulls) came back in and forced the prices up.

Ch 2. Trading Signals

Having spent years researching and back testing many trading indicators and hundreds of combinations of indicators I can tell you some good news:

Some technical indicators work some of the time.

That's the best news I can give you, I am afraid. Trading signals do not work all of the time, or even most of the time.

The bad news is there is no way of telling which indicator is going to work at what time and in what situation. Indicators are, necessarily, describing what has already happened not what is going to happen. But traders keep on using them as though they could predict the future, and this is what gives us an advantage.

If we know what people are going to do, based on the indicators, then we have a good indication of what the market is going to do.

If we know that traders watch the 50-day moving average and we see the stock price fall through that then we know that further falls are likely because traders see this as an indication that it will continue to fall. In other words, it is a self-fulfilling prophecy.

For those of you who have been following my blog (HeatherCullen.com/Blog) you will know that in 2021 we were following the S&P 500 ETF SPY, and that one of the trading signals we were monitoring was the 50 day SMA (Simple moving average, explained in Chapter 4). SPY bounced off the 50 day SMA no less than six times during the year!

The best that can be said of trading signals is that some of them work some of the time. There is no fool-proof signal that always works, and we don't know under what circumstances which signals are going to work. You might wonder why anyone uses them if we don't know if and when it is going to work, and that is a very good question. The correct answer is:

Because traders who are trading the signals think they are important and make their decisions based on them.

If we think of the stock market as millions of people all looking at the same stocks and the same data, we get a better idea of how to trade it. You can never predict what one person is going to do, but by looking at what has happened in the past you can make a reasonable prediction about what they are going to do in the future.

If we take a medical analogy, it becomes clearer. You can't predict whether an individual is going to get cancer over the next year, but if you take 100,000 people you can predict with reasonable certainty that around 500 will be affected.

It's the same with the stock market; you can't predict what an individual trader will do, but you can often predict what a lot of them will do. So, back to trading signals. Why are they important? *Because traders THINK they are important.*

And when they think something is important then they act on it and so by watching the trading signals we can often predict what traders are going to do. So, let's go through some signals that you may want to use.

Chart Drawing Tools

Firstly, we will look at the signals that you don't have to calculate, you simply draw them on a stock chart. The drawing tools we are going to review are:

> ➢ Support & Resistance
> ➢ Support & Resistance Channels
> ➢ Trend lines
> ➢ Trading Channels

Support and Resistance

Support and resistance lines are one of the most commonly used signals, both for individual stocks and ETFs.

The **Support Line** is simply a horizontal line drawn on a chart which shows the price under which a stock is unlikely to fall. The stock price is 'supported' at this level, as every time it falls towards that level it moves back up again.

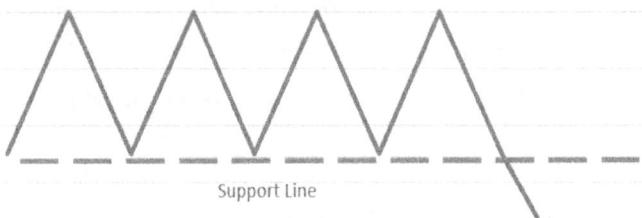

Support Line

What is happening is that as the price of the stock falls traders notice and start to think that the stock is getting 'cheap' and 'good value', so they start to buy. This forces the price up away from the support line.

This human behavior can be seen in any buying situation, whether real estate, cars, clothes, whatever. There is always a price where the potential buyer thinks 'that's too good a bargain to miss', and moves in to buy it.

If the support line is broken and the stock starts to trade under it, this is a bearish sign. Traders have no idea when the price may stop falling, so they often dump the stocks, accelerating the falls. A 'break in support' (trading moves under the support line) means that traders think that it is time to sell the stock.

The **Resistance Line** is exactly the opposite. It's where traders think that the stock looks 'expensive' and are not willing to buy if it is over that price. Traders who own the stock get nervous and start to sell their holdings, and as there are few buyers that means the price goes down. Every time the stock gets to that level it falters and then starts falling as buyers melt away.

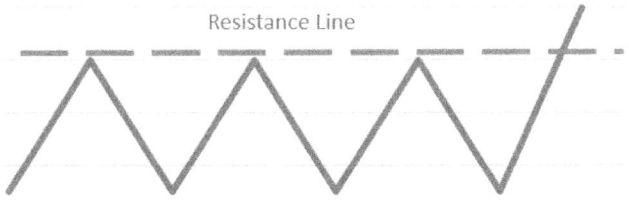

Sooner or later (usually) it gets through this resistance line and that is a bullish sign that it now has enough momentum to keep going up, for a while at least.

This is one of the signals that traders use to enter a stock trade as once it breaks through resistance it often continues to go up for some time. This is termed a 'breakout' and traders are always looking for these as a signal to get into the market.

Trend lines

Trend lines are simply straight lines that are drawn on a chart to show which way the stock has been going. The words 'has been' are significant. The reason we draw trend lines is that we are assuming (or hoping) that the stock will continue along the trend line so that we know where it is going and can trade accordingly.

Now we already know that no-one can say what a stock is going to do tomorrow, next week, next month, next year. But the good news is that they often follow the trend lines – that is, until they don't!

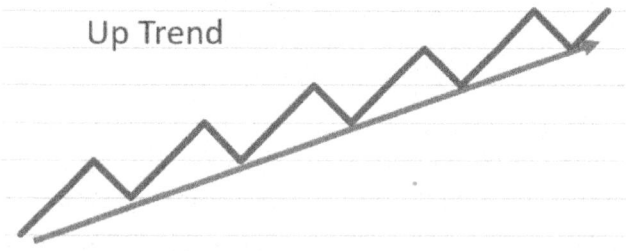

Up Trend

There are rules for drawing trend lines. They are:

- ➢ Uptrend trend lines are drawn connecting 2 or more LOW points.

- ➢ Downtrend trend lines are drawn connecting 2 or more HIGH points.

- ➢ At least 3 points must be connected for a trend line to be VALID.

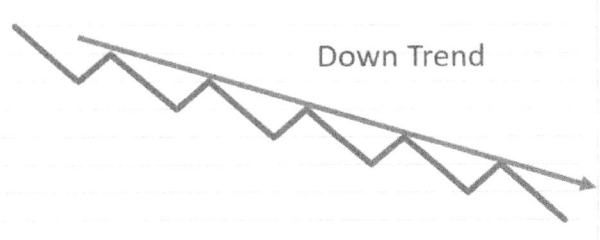

Down Trend

When you start to look at charts, drawing in the trend lines is good to do because it takes away all the noise. By noise, we mean the daily ups and downs that are part of normal stock movement. They happen constantly, and are what I refer to as the 'waves', You can't tell whether the tide is going in or out if you only look at a few waves, but if you watch 100 waves then you will have a very good idea which direction it is going.

Trend lines also make you look at the chart and see what is actually there, and not you think should be there, or have read online that morning or that someone has told you. As we mentioned before, keeping a clear head is absolutely vital to being successful. Listening to others is almost always guaranteed to bring you to a sticky end.

Trend lines are sometimes described as 'lines of least resistance'. In other words, if a stock is going up then that is the easiest thing for that stock to keep on going up. To change the upward trend something must happen to change traders' point of view about the stock. That could be something that affects the whole market (like a recession, or inflation getting out of control) or it could be stock specific (all the executives were in the same plane, and it crashed. That actually happened, just google Sundance Resources plane crash).

Trading Channels

Trend lines often give us trading channels which are just like support and resistance lines except that they are not horizontal.

Every time the stock gets to the bottom of the channel it looks 'cheap' or 'good value' and buyers step in, forcing the price up.

When it gets to the top trend line then traders start to think that it is 'expensive' or 'toppy' and start to sell, moving the price down, away from the line. It will keep going in that channel until something changes the traders' minds about the stock.

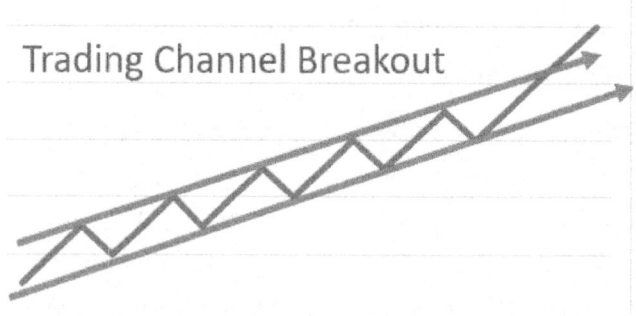

Trading Channel Breakout

When the stock breaks out of the trading channel that is significant, just like the support and resistance we talked of earlier. If it breaks out of the top of the channel, then this is bullish, and it is likely to keep going up for a while at least. If it drops through the bottom of the channel then this is considered to be bearish and traders will dump their positions, adding to the decline in prices.

It is also quite normal behavior to then retest by retracing to the top channel line and then bounce off again. The top channel line then becomes the bottom channel line of the new channel. The same is true, in reverse, if it breaks out of the bottom of the trading channel.

If you google to read more about this, you will see that the next thing they usually start talking about is putting the vertical axes on a logarithmic scale. Ignore this. It does not help. They are just trying to sound smart. The further you get away from the actual data the more you can persuade yourself that you see things that are not really there, and the more mistakes you will make. Usually costly mistakes. And we don't want that!

52-Week High

This is really a version of resistance. The 52-week high is the highest price at which a stock has traded during the past year and has a psychological effect on traders. You will often see it referred to in the financial press as though it were some mystical event; just google '52 week high' and look at the news tab to see the headlines.

However, traders think that it is important and so it can become a major point of resistance. Reaching a 52 week high should be a good sign that everything is going well for the stock, but traders are a jumpy lot and tend to overreact. They often sell, pushing the stock price down away from the high.

If, on the other hand, it pushes through the high (for example, if there was a good announcement about future prospects, or great reporting results) then this is seen as a very bullish sign and traders pile in, driving it up further.

Ch 3. Subjective & Objective

It is important to distinguish between subjective indicators and objective indicators, in other words subjective indicators where different traders will see different things and objective indicators that are calculated using a formula.

We have seen that drawing trend lines has rules. This may seem objective, but indicators drawn by traders are subject to the drawer's bias. The interpretation of price movements and where the trend lines are drawn is influenced by the drawer's perspective, experience and cognitive biases.

Confirmation bias is the human tendency to search for and interpret information in a way that supports their beliefs, and ignore information that contradicts these beliefs. It has been referred to as an internal 'yes man'. Even if two traders have the same information, they can interpret it in different ways.

If a trader has invested in a stock, naturally they want to see it go up, so they will unconsciously search for information that supports this belief, and ignore any information to the contrary. They don't do this intentionally, of course, they are not aware of their bias.

Many people think that this is the biggest mistake made by both professional and individual investors. Traders tend to look for confirming evidence rather than evaluating all available information. It is a natural human tendency; we all do it and not just in trading. If we think the market is bullish (going up) we look for evidence to support that and dismiss evidence that would prove us wrong. It is always good to ask yourself 'What if I am wrong?' and make sure that you can live with the consequences.

Drawing lines on a chart has a human bias. For example, when you draw in a trend line even if you follow the rules two people can draw it differently. In the old days when people used to use paper charts the advice was to turn the chart upside down and draw in the trend lines. That was you are more likely to see what is actually there rather than you think should be there.

I have yet to come across a charting package that enables you to vertically flip a chart, so that particular way of avoiding unconscious bias is not available to us. We will have to content ourselves with asking *'what if I am wrong?'*

For example, look at the following charts. Both are of the S&P 500 over the same period in 2023. Both have trend lines drawn following the rules, but one has one line, the other three.

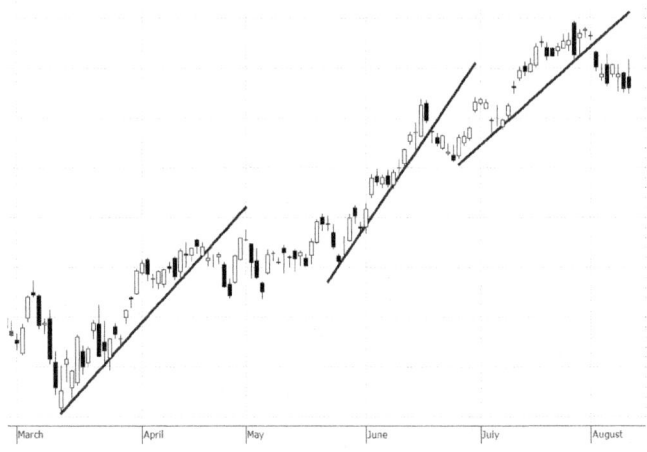

Which is correct? Technically, both are which shows the unconscious human bias that we all bring to trading even following the rules.

Where you start drawing the line has an enormous effect on where the line is drawn, as is the period you are drawing it over. In the first example, if it were the end of April, you would draw a trend line that would clearly show that the uptrend had been broken. However, that is disproved when after trading sideways during late April and May, SPX resumed the uptrend, which was broken at mid-June. After a short downturn, it started another uptrend which finished at the end of July.

There is no way that you would have drawn the trend line that you see in the second chart, because it wasn't obvious then – but it is now. Be aware that you may be missing the bigger picture. It is good to condense your chart, for example by changing the setting to weekly so that you can see if the current trend is part of a longer term trend.

Hindsight is a wonderful thing; it enables you to get everything right. That's why so many people use it when they are writing books!

Calculated Indicators

Calculated indicators are created by using a formula on price data. They are mathematically computed, so everyone with the same data will get the same result when they calculate them. However, this does not mean that everyone will interpret the data in the same way; they don't.

This is where subjectivity and confirmation bias creep in again. The actual indicator is objectively calculated but the interpretation is subjective.

Calculated indicators are usually superimposed on the price chart. You never have to calculate any of these indicators yourself as practically all graphing packages, both free and paid, will do this for you. Some of the indicators we will look at are:

- ➤ Moving Averages, Death and Golden Crosses
- ➤ Moving Average Convergence Divergence (MACD)
- ➤ Volume and On Balance Volume (OBV)
- ➤ Relative Strength Indicator (RSI)
- ➤ Bollinger Bands
- ➤ Fibonacci Retracements

Ch 4. Moving Averages

One of the most widely used indicators is the moving average. This is a time series analysis, a statistical calculation that smooths out fluctuations in a price chart, enabling us to better see the trend. In other words, it is easier to see the tide rather than be distracted by the waves.

A moving average is usually referred to as an 'MA'. They calculated by adding the new value (the latest one) and taking away an old value (the oldest one). Don't worry about doing the calculations yourself. Any charting software will do it for you.

We can have moving averages of different time periods, like 10-day MAs, 50-day MAs, or 1-month MAs. In general, the longer the time period, the smoother the MA line. Shorter period MAs fluctuate more than longer period MAs so look 'choppier'.

On the next page is a chart of SPY (the ETF that tracks the S&P 500) with a 10-day moving average (thin) and a 200-day (thick) moving average. You can see that both MAs smooth out some of the noise so that you can see the trend more easily. Using a 10-day MA smooths a bit, but the 200-day MA smooths out even more.

The disadvantage of the 200-day SMA is that it takes longer to respond. You can see that after the prices start to decrease at the end of July the 10-day SMA reflects this, but the 200-day SMA is still going up.

It is important that you get the concept of a moving average, and what it does. Essentially it smooths out the stock graph, eliminating the noise and enabling you to see the real movement. In other words, to see the tide, not the waves.

The MA we have described above is often referred to as an SMA – a 'Simple Moving Average', where all the prices in the time period are given equal weighting.

The word 'simple' implies that there is a more complex moving average. Of course, there is! Remember, this is trading – if anything can be made more complicated, it will be. Exponentially!

Exponential Moving Averages

The term EMA means 'Exponential Moving Average', and it gives more weight to the more recent prices. Unlike the SMA which weights the prices equally, the EMA applies exponentially decreasing weights to older prices.

This means that the most recent prices contribute more significantly to the average, which makes an EMA more responsive to recent changes in the market. This seems logical. What happened yesterday should carry more weight that what happened 2 weeks ago, and this is what the EMA does for you.

Again, you don't have to know how to calculate it, any charting package or website will do that for you. Just choose EMA and the time period that you want.

Which one should we use?

Both have a place. If we are trying to predict what the market is going to do, then I suggest that you use the SMA. Why? Because that is what most traders watch and act on, and we are trying to predict what they are going to do.

However, I think that the EMA gives a truer picture of what is actually happening. So, which one? I watch both. Often there is not a lot of difference, but sometimes it is significant.

Three of the most widely used are the 50-day SMA, 100-day SMA and the 200-day SMA. In fact, they are so widely followed you sometimes see them in news headlines, more often for bearish stories:

'DOW drops through 50-Day Moving Average.'

than bullish stories:

'DOW bounces off 50-day Moving Average'.

If a stock or index is approaching one of these moving averages, you can be sure that there are a lot of traders watching it and holding off making their decisions until they know what it is going to do when it reaches it.

Death and Golden Crosses

While individual moving averages are watched, how they interact with each other is watched even more closely. As we know, we can put the 50, 100 and 200-day moving averages on a single chart. The 200-day one will be smoother than the 100-day SMA, which in turn will be smoother than the 50-day.

At some point the moving averages will cross, and this is a trading signal that traders watch out for. These crosses are very flamboyantly named:

> **Death Cross.** If the short term MA crosses below the longer term MA, then this is a very bearish sign called a Death Cross or Dead Cross.

➢ **Golden Cross.** If the short term MA crosses above the longer term MA, then this is a very bullish sign called a Golden Cross.

Lagging indicators

Moving averages are considered lagging indicators because they are calculated on past prices and may not reflect the current market. Instead, they confirm a trend that has already begun.

This is true for golden and death crosses also. The amount that they lag depends on the time period used for calculating the MA. For example, the 5-day / 10-day cross will lag less than the 100-day / 200-day cross.

Here are the 10-day and 200-day SMAs during the Covid crisis:

SPY 2020

Death Cross

200-day SMA

10-day SMA

Golden Cross

2020 | February | March | April | May | June

➢ In early March, the 10-day SMA crossed over the 200 SMA causing a death cross.

➢ In early June, the 10-day SMA crossed over the 200 SMA causing a death cross.

Entry and exit signals

Traders use the death and golden crosses as entry and exit signals. There are no standard parameters, but the most traders use the 50 / 200 SMA crosses.

Entry signal.

➢ Golden cross. When traders see a golden cross, they tend to behave in a bullish way by buying, which will push the price up even further.

Exit signal.

➢ **Death cross.** When traders see a death cross, they tend to behave in a bearish way by selling down their holdings, which will push the market down even further.

Ch 5. The MACD

The MACD is one of the most commonly used technical indicators and is also one of the easiest to understand. It is an acronym of:

M – Moving

A – Average

C – Convergence

D – Divergence

It belongs to a class of technical analysis tools called Oscillators. This means that it is an indicator that oscillates either between 2 fixed levels or simply above and below a center line.

Some other oscillators are the RSI (Relative Strength Index), the Stochastic Oscillator, the True Strength Index and the Ultimate Oscillator.

Although the MACD is classified as an oscillator because its values rise and fall around a zero line, it is slightly different to other oscillators because the scale is not normalized to a limited range. It has no upper or lower limits.

The reason is simple. The MACD is created from moving averages, and the value of the moving average depends on the stock price.

➢ The most expensive stock on the NYSE (New York Stock Exchange) is Berkshire Hathaway. One share will cost you $544,000, and in the last year its MACD has been in the range (-8,000, +8,000)

➢ Ford Motor Company has a share price of around $10, so its MACD is in the range (-0.55, +0.70)

Of course, this can be normalized by dividing share price by the MACD value, but this is not generally done. The MACD measures how fast a particular market is moving. It also tries to pinpoint turning points when the stock is changing direction. What is interesting about the MACD is the large variations in the way traders interpret and use it. Different traders use it in completely different ways.

Calculating the MACD

There are 3 components of the MACD, and their names are not at all helpful:

➢ MACD Graph
➢ MACD Line
➢ MACD Histogram

Confusingly, the graph and the line are both lines on a graph. Baffled? So am I. You have to wonder: who thought up these names? Is this really the best they could come up with? Luckily the histogram is easy to identify. Here is what the MACD looks like:

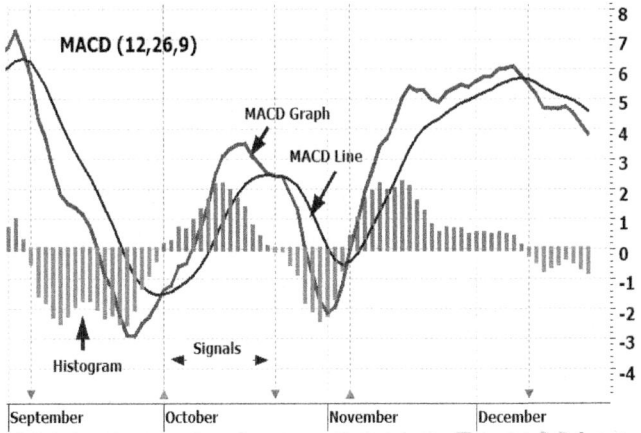

The MACD is never graphed on the same chart as the price chart like SMAs are. Instead, it is always in a separate chart, usually below the price chart.

MACD Parameters

The MACD has 3 parameters, and the most common parameters are written MACD (12, 26, 9). Other parameters can be used but these are the standard ones that most traders use.

They seem like rather strange numbers, but they derive from the days before online trading and charting when only paper daily charts were the norm. Then, they could not get the up to the minute online charts that we take for granted now.

It is often claimed that the parameters 12, 26, 9 are chosen because they are the most effective. This is incorrect. The reason we use them is historical. At the time the MACD was developed the working week was 6 days so the (12,26,9) settings are for 2 weeks, 1 month and 9 days (one and a half weeks).

These parameters have nothing to do with the best performance. However, these are the 'standard' parameters and traders will be watching them and making trading decisions based on them so, as for moving averages, it becomes a self-fulfilling prophecy.

Of course, changing the parameters can be done easily in most charting packages, and there is a case to be made for updating them to suit our current ways of trading, but we must think of the crowd psychology in play here. If most traders are using the standard parameters, then their actions will be in line with what they are observing.

If the MACD gives a down signal, then you can be sure that a lot of traders see that and will close bullish positions and start bearish strategies pushing prices down even further and confirming the downward trend.

It is the same as prices falling through a support line or push up through a resistance line tends to trigger traders into actions which exacerbate the trend.

Calculating the MACD

Most charting packages offer the MACD as a standard indicator so all you need to do is tick a box and it gets drawn for you, but knowing how it is calculated is useful to your understanding of it.

➤ **MACD Graph**: calculated by subtracting the 12 day EMA from the 26 day EMA.

➤ **MACD line:** a 9 day EMA of the MACD graph.

➤ **MACD Histogram** is the difference between the MACD graph and the MACD line.

As we have noted the terminology sounds confusing, but a MACD chart is actually very easy to read. The histogram is easily recognizable, the smoother of the two lines is the MACD line and the more volatile line is the MACD graph.

The MACD Graph is sometimes called the 'signal line', but that introduces even more confusion because the vertical lines that signal the histogram crossing the zero line are also called signal lines. Confused? Understandable.

MACD entry and exit signals

As I mentioned before, the ways that traders use the MACD vary rather a lot. The way that many use it is for entry and exit signals for a trade. They use one or more of:

Entry Signal

➢ MACD graph crosses the MACD line from below

➢ Both the graph and the line are trending up

➢ The histogram is trending up.

Exit Signal

➢ MACD graph crosses the MACD line from above

➢ Both the graph and the line are trending down

➢ The histogram is trending down.

Here's a real life example of the MACD on the SPY Chart during the 2020 Covid bear market:

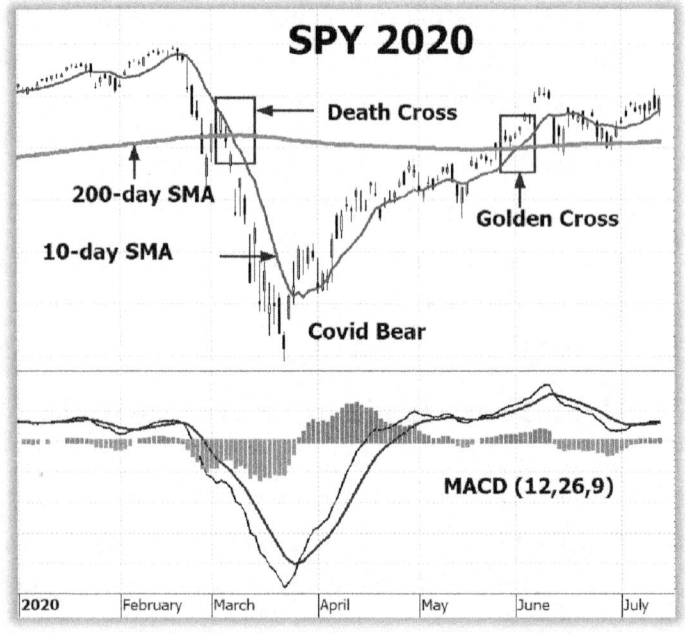

A MACD bearish signal happened on 21 February, several days before the actual 12/26 death cross on 27 February. In other words, the MACD was a leading indicator warning us of a change in trend that was coming, a week before it was obvious on the price chart.

Likewise, on 26 March we get a MACD bullish signal, which happens before the actual 12/26 golden cross on 9 April. Again, the MACD is a leading indicator, telling us what is going to happen.

Is the MACD the ultimate signal? Unfortunately, no. Here is an example of the SPY in 2021 where the market was trending up very steadily, but in that time the MACD generated 12 bullish and 11 bearish signals. If we had been trading on these we would have been whipsawed in and out of trades.

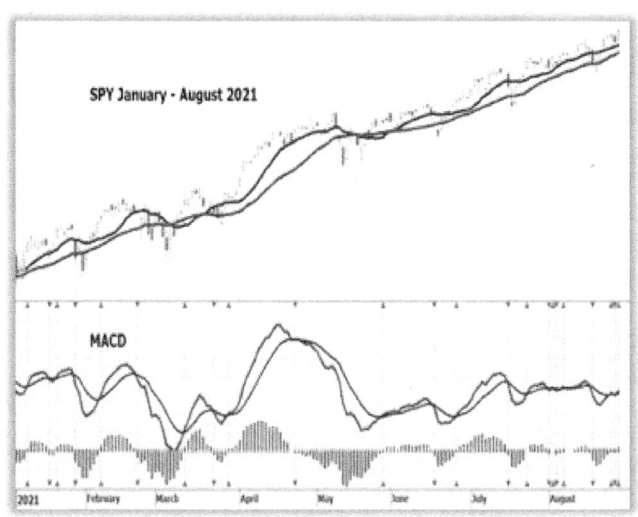

Returning to the Covid bear, in my book **In The Money: Bear Market Strategy** we look at what happened next. We saw the MACD give several false signals, which would have resulted in several losing trades. We looked at why the MACD worked in this case but not in other cases.

I have personally backtested it to 1927 and found that if you traded using the MACD signals you underperformed the market by 65%. Not a happy result! As with all indicators sometimes it works, sometimes it doesn't.

Ch 6. On Balance Volume

Volume is important, and I encourage you to have it at the bottom of every chart you are looking at, along with the moving average of the volume as it measures the conviction of traders. And the strength of the price movement.

If, for example, the price of a stock jumps and it has well above average volume then that movement is more significant than the same jump if the volume were low.

SPY 2020

Volume is usually graphed at the bottom of a stock chart. You will notice that on sudden declines the volumes increase enormously as traders scramble to dump their positions before the price goes even lower. Traders are a volatile lot!

In the chart above, you can see what happened during the Covid bear market. As the prices plummeted, the volume increased hugely. On the recovery, the volumes we up compared with pre-covid, but not as large as during the first phase of the bear.

On Balance Volume

On Balance Volume (OBV) measures buying and selling pressure and, like volume itself, is graphed below the price chart.

The **OBV** is calculated by adding the day's volume to a cumulative total when the stock price closes up and subtracting the day's volume when the stock price closes down. Again, you do not have to calculate it; your graphing software will do that for you.

The actual value of OBV is not important, it is the direction that it is going in that you take notice of. The chart below is an example of the OBV during the Covid bear market, using the stock AAPL (Apple). You can see that the trend and the OBV are mostly in synch. When one goes down so does the other and the reverse is also true. Except when it doesn't, that is the trading signal.

If the OBV is increasing yet the stock price stays flat. It indicates that money is moving into the stock, but the stock hasn't reacted - yet.

The theory is that volume precedes prices and that when there is increased volume without a corresponding price movement then this has a 'spring' effect, so that when the pressure is built up then the stock will eventually react with a lot of momentum.

Does it work? Sometimes it does. Sometimes it doesn't. Just like all indicators!

OBV Entry and Exit Signals

There are several ways that traders use OBV. If OBV and prices are moving in the same direction, then this confirms an existing trend. Divergence, on the other hand, gives the entry and exit signals. When the OBV diverges from the price movement then this is a signal.

Entry Signal

> ➢ If prices and making new lows but OBV is moving higher then this is an entry signal.

Exit Signal

> ➢ If prices and making new highs but OBV is moving lower, then this is an exit signal.

Ch 7. RSI (Relative Strength)

The **Relative Strength Indicator (RSI)** is a momentum indicator (momentum is the rate of the rise or fall in prices) and is used by traders to ascertain the strength of changes in the stock price. It is plotted below the price chart and looks like this:

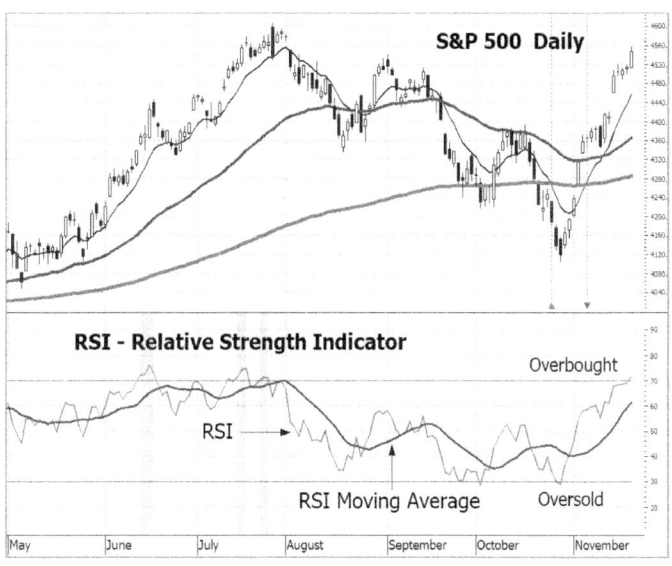

The chart above is the S&P 500 earlier this year (2023). The RSI can is plotted below the main chart, and the right axis ranges from 0 – 100. The RSI oscillates between these 2 values, hence its classification as an **oscillator**. There are two horizontal lines, typically at 30 and 70. When the RSI is above 70 this means that the stock is overbought, and so likely to go down, and when it is below 30 then it is oversold, and so likely to go up.

The typical settings are for a 14 day period, but this can be changed depending on the timeframe you are looking at. It is common to also put a moving average on the RSI to help smooth out the noise so that you can see what it is doing.

In the chart on the previous page the more volatile line is the RSI and the smoother line is the moving average of the RSI.

RSI Entry and Exit Signals

Entry Signal

> ➢ Traders use the RSI passing into the overbought area as a signal to get out of a trade as they think that the price is likely to go up.

Exit Signal

> ➢ Traders use the RSI passing into the oversold area as a signal to get out of a trade as they think that the price is likely to go down.

Does it work? As with all indicators, sometimes it does and sometimes it doesn't. This time it worked.

RSI Example: S&P 500

In the daily graph of the S&P 500 below, you can see that in June and again in July the RSI moved into overbought territory, and in July it was followed by the moving average at the 70 level also.

This preceded the downturn which started in August and ended late October. You can also see that twice in October we touched, but didn't quite cross over into oversold territory, but the market went up anyway.

Does the market always go down after the RSI is in overbought territory? No, the RSI can stay overbought (or oversold) for some time. Take a look at this graph, also of the S&P 500 during the Covid bear market.

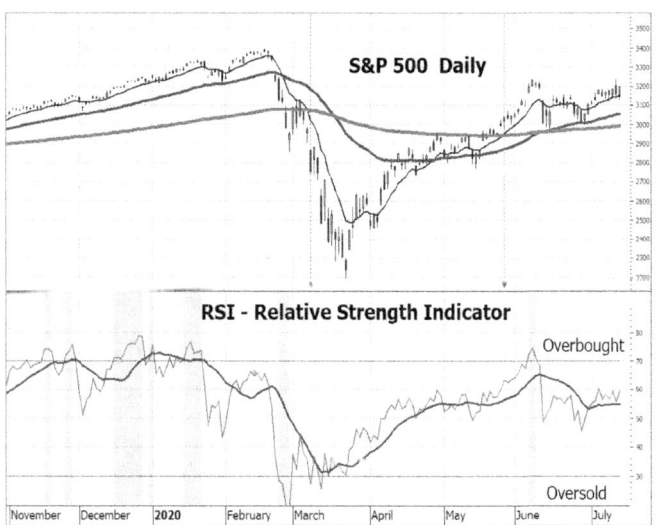

You can see that prior to the drop in prices there were extended periods when it was in overbought territory. It stayed there for most of December 2019 and this was not followed by a downturn. It was in overbought again in January, and this time it did precede a downturn, but it was very minor, more of a blip than a dip. If you had sold your shares on either of these signals you would probably be regretting it.

Next, you can see that it dropped into oversold right at the start of the bear market. This is a buy signal, and you would have bought in just as the market was going to drop another 22%. Not a great result! This highlights the dangers of trusting in indicators without back testing to see if they actually work.

There are many books showing charts with perfectly-aligned signals and price action, but you can be sure that these examples are selected because they were one of the situations where it worked. There are few books that show you instances of indicators not working.

The takeaway for the RSI? As for all indicators, sometimes it works, sometimes it doesn't. The trouble is we don't know when it is going to work and when it isn't. Such is life!

Ch 8. Bollinger Bands

Bollinger **Bands** are not a champagne orchestra, unfortunately. Sounds like fun, but no. They are nothing to do with the 200 year old French champagne house, but are a technical indicator invented in the 1980s by John Bollinger.

Like the RSI, Bollinger bands are designed to determine if a stock is overbought or oversold. Unlike RSI it is plotted on top of the price chart. Bollinger bands consist of three lines:

➤ **SMA** - the center trend line is the simple moving average, usually a 20 day period.

➤ **Upper Band:** this is a line drawn two standard deviations above the SMA.

➤ **Lower Band:** This is a line drawn two standard deviations below the SMA.

The theory is that as the price approaches the upper band the stock is oversold, and when approaching the lower band, it is overbought. Practically, that means that touching the lower band is a buy signal and the upper band is a sell signal.

Below is an example of Bollinger Bands on the stock AAPL (Apple) over the last four months. You can immediately see a problem:

The bands expand and contract depending on the volatility of the stock price.

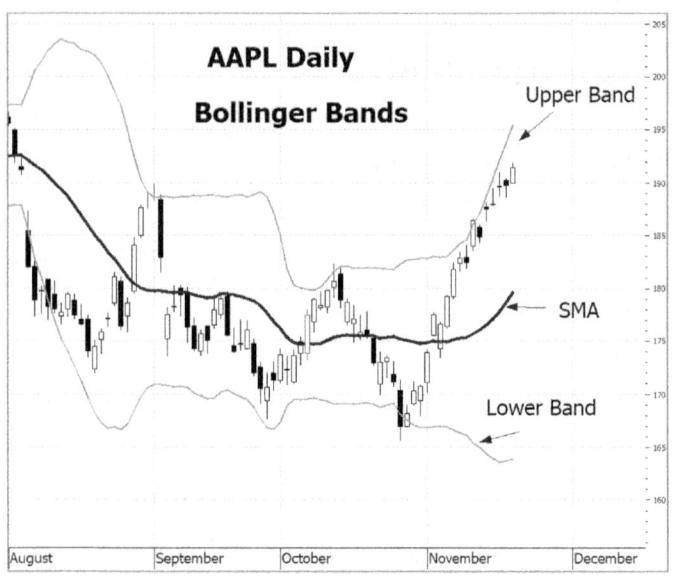

A standard deviation quantifies the variation in prices, by measuring how far they are from the mean (average). Normally, 95% of the data falls between 2 standard deviations up and 2 down. In other words, only 2.5% of prices are above the upper band and 2.5% below the lower band.

You can see that in October the bands were relatively close together, only around $20 apart. However, today (November 21st) they are more widely separated, around $43 apart. This is to be expected from any indicator using standard deviations. If a dataset has little variability, then the standard deviation is small.

For example, a class of third graders might have an average age of 8 years with a standard deviation of 6 months. But, if we included the whole school the average age might still be 8 years, but the standard deviation would be much bigger, say 2 years.

In the chart above, Bollinger bands seem to be working quite well. After touching the upper band at the end of August it did indeed drop to below the SMA, as it did also in mid-October. Conversely, in late September and in late October it touched the bottom band, both of which signaled a rise in prices.

Bollinger Bands Example

They worked between August and October. But what about the rest of 2023? Let's check the chart:

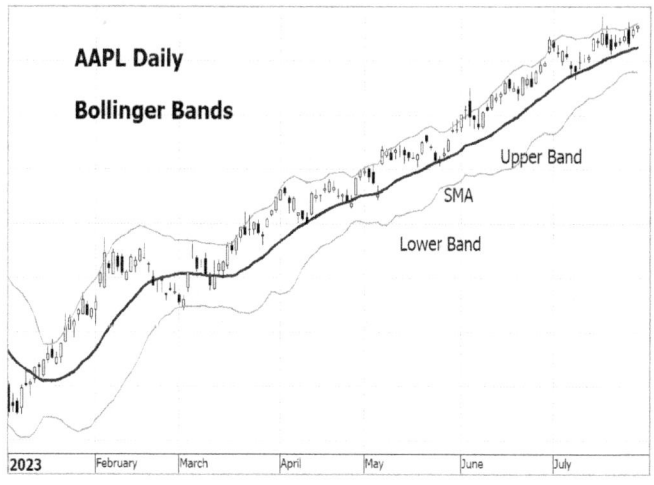

Not such a good performance here! You can see that it spent most of the time **above** the SMA and often touched the upper band. On a quick count, almost 50 candlesticks touched it. Which one of those 50 should we use as our signal?

So, what about using Bollinger bands for our entry and exit signals? I find them interesting as a description of what has gone on in the past (i.e., a lagging indicator) but not at all useful in determining the direction of the stock, far less predicting changes in direction.

However, many traders swear by them, and act on them, so we have to notice them if we are trying to predict stock behavior.

Entry and Exit Signals

Entry Signal

> ➢ Traders use the price hitting the lower Bollinger band RSI as a signal to get into a trade as they think that the price is likely to go up.

Exit Signal

> ➢ Traders use the price hitting the upper Bollinger band RSI as a signal to get out of a trade as they think that the price is likely to go down.

Ch 9. Average True Range

Average **True Range** (ATR) is included simply because it is one of the most commonly used indicators. It is not particularly helpful in determining when to enter or exit a trade.

The ATR is a measure of volatility, and shows potential price fluctuations. It is not a directional indicator; in that it doesn't help you decide which way the trend is going.

Instead, it quantifies the magnitude of price changes. Which, to be fair, you would probably already have worked out yourself without needing an indicator! However, traders use it so let's go through what it is.

Calculating the ATR

The ATR calculates the average range between high and low prices over a period, usually 14 days. The ATR indicator is the greater of one of:

> ➢ Current high less the current low;

> ➢ Absolute value of current high less previous close;

> ➢ Absolute value of current low less previous close.

The ATR is then a moving average and is graphed below the stock chart. As usual, it is calculated by your graphing package, which is just as well as the formula is very fiddly because of all the possibilities.

When the stock has high volatility then the ATR is high, and when there is low volatility, it is low. ATR does not provide specific entry or exit signals, but traders use it in the different ways.

Entry Signal.

> **Breakout trading:** if the price surpasses a recent high or low by a multiple of the ATR then you trade in the direction of the breakout.

Exit Signal

> **Stops** - set stop loss levels, e.g. exit when the price is more than 2 times the ATR below the entry price.

My recommendation is to ignore the ATR as it is of no practical purpose and its use is so subjective.

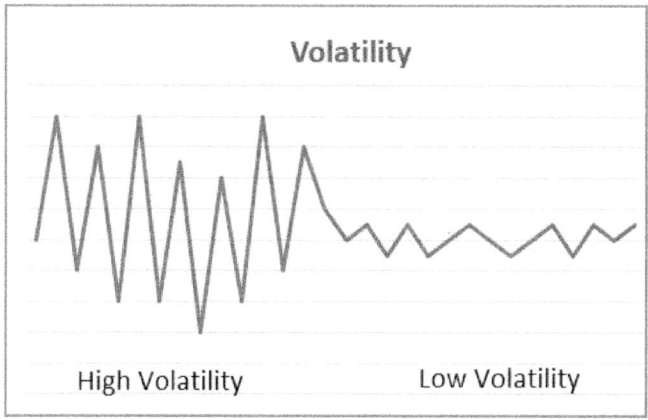

It is better to look at a chart to see if the stock is in a period of high volatility or low volatility.

Why make things complicated when there is no actual advantage?

Ch 10. Fibonacci Retracement

Fibonacci **Retracement** is an indicator that is beloved by many traders. Personally, I find it a bit 'woo-woo'. You'll see what I mean.

The story starts well. The Fibonacci sequence is a series of numbers, where each number is the sum of the previous two numbers. Starting with 0 and 1, the sequence goes: 0, 1, 1, 2, 3, 5, 8, 13, 21, 34, and so on to infinity.

Fibonacci No	Ratio
0	
1	
1	1.000000
2	2.000000
3	1.500000
5	1.666667
8	1.600000
13	1.625000
21	1.615385
34	1.619048
55	1.617647
89	1.618182
144	1.617978
233	1.618056
377	1.618026
610	1.618037
987	1.618033
1597	1.618034
2584	1.618034
4181	1.618034

In Fibonacci retracement, the key levels are derived from the ratios between the numbers.

If we divide any of the numbers in the series by the previous number, the ratio is approximately 1.618. In other words, each number is roughly 1.618 times its predecessor, or to put it another way each number is 61.8% of the value of the next number in the series.

The golden ratio is found many times in nature, like the number of petals on a flower, seashells, hurricanes, and galaxies – even human faces. It is quite fascinating (just google 'Fibonacci in nature') and you will see some excellent photos illustrating it. But what has it to do with trading?

This is where it gets a bit murky. Possibly it doesn't have anything to do with trading at all, but many traders **think** that it does. Because they think that it does, they act upon it, which means that it becomes important if you are trying to predict market behavior.

The 'Magic' Numbers

This ratio of 1.618 is known as the golden ratio. Traders use this ratio, or rather its inverse, 61.8% as a 'magic' number. That is along with some other 'magic' numbers.

- **38.2%,** which is derived from dividing a number with the number two along from it in the series.

- **23.6%,** which is derived from dividing a number with the number three along from it in the series.

- **50%,** which has nothing to do with the Fibonacci series, but is chosen because traders think that there is a tendency of prices to continue in a particular direction after a 50% retracement.

Some traders think that these numbers help them predict the extent of any market or stock retracements using the magic numbers are 23.6%, 38.2%, 50%, 61.8% and 100%. If you take 2 extreme points on a stock chart (i.e., a peak and a trough) and draw horizontal lines at these levels you will find the support and resistance levels.

Fibonacci devotees will point to any number of charts where the Fibonacci levels are where the stock price reversed. Does it work? I have yet to see it work consistently. I have seen it retrofitted to stock movements many times, but I have not seen it successfully used as a predictor.

Is it useful? Only after the fact. We don't know the peak and the trough until afterwards, so what we are describing is a lagging indicator.

Fibonacci retracements, in my opinion, are more in the eye of the beholder than in actual fact. However, this is just my opinion, and you will find many traders who swear by them. Let's look at an example:

Here is SPY during the Covid Bear of 2020. I have drawn in the Fibonacci Retracements. None of them look particularly significant to me, but possibly I am biased and don't want to see what is obvious to everyone!

Humans tend to see what they want to see so possibly I can't see a pattern that is actually there – or possibly using the Fibonacci Retracement indicator results in quite a few cases of temporary traders!

Entry and Exit Signals

Using Fibonacci retracement for trading is not as clear-cut as for other signals. Here's what you have to do in an uptrend:

- Identify a trend where there are clear highs and lows.
- Choose a low (trough) and a high (peak).
- Draw the Fibonacci retracement levels from the low to the high.
- The retracement levels are potential support / resistance.

Entry Signal

- Traders use the price going through support as a signal to get into a trade as they think that the price is likely to go up.

Exit Signal

- Traders use the price bouncing off a resistance level as a signal to get out of a trade as they think that the price is likely to go down.

**Reverse all the above signals if you are in
a downtrend.**

i.e. in a downtrend draw the retracement levels
starting from the high and going to the low, etc.

Helpful hint: If you can't find the Fibonacci
Retracement in your charting package indicators, try
looking in the drawing tools.

Epilogue

There are hundreds of technical indicators that you can use to analyze stock charts; and we have looked at some of the most common ones.

If you think about it, there is very little market data available to base these indicators on, just OHLCV (Open, High, Low, Close, Volume). While there are hundreds of technical indicators, they are all necessarily based on this data.

The drawback of relying on technical indicators is that it provides an Illusion of Certainty. Using technical indicators gives a sense of certainty and predictability, which is often misplaced creating a false sense of security. It is good to remember:

**Technical Indicators work some,
but not all, of the time.**

The problem is, we don't know when they are going to work and when they are not. Most stock market books carefully select charts where they worked and show this as 'proof'. I have tried to show situations where they worked, and also where they didn't.

Having said that you can't possibly be successful as a trader without being able to read stock charts. The trick is to always be aware of their limitations and be prepared, always, to ask yourself what if I am wrong? And make sure that you can live with the consequences and have a plan of what you are going to do. This 100 years old quote is still relevant today:

The principles of successful stock speculation are based on the supposition that people will continue in the future to make the mistakes that they have made in the past. (Edwin Lefevre)

As it turns out people DO continue to make the same mistakes they always have, and the only way to see these mistakes is by analyzing charts to see what has happened in the past, and figuring out what is most likely to happen in the future. Being able to read stock charts is the essential tool you need to be able to do this.

I've been trading now for over 25 years, and find it endlessly fascinating. The independence it gives me makes for a great life for which I am very grateful, and I highly recommend it.

May your trading be successful, rewarding – and enjoyable.

Heather

November 2023

About the Author
Heather Cullen

Heather wrote her book series In The Money and The One Hour Expert based on her 25 years of experience in the stock market. During these years, she made hundreds of mistakes but managed to survive and finally to become a successful investor.

Through the early years, while keeping her day job as an IT Director, she was learning and trading every night. She read every book she could find on trading strategy and psychology, paid for numerous courses, subscribed to hundreds of newsletters and websites, tried every crackpot theory, and fell for the stories of every financial guru who claimed to be making millions before breakfast.

But none of the 'trading secrets' worked more than occasionally, and the financial freedom she so desperately wanted proved to be elusive. Giving up her day job seemed like an unattainable dream.

Winning and Losing

Over the first 15 years of trading, she made money and then lost it again. So many times! Never enough to wipe her out completely, but she wasn't able to throw up her day job and live the life of her dreams.

Although she put in many long hours of research, monitoring, and back-testing she was never consistently successful. Slowly, she realized that hard work alone did not lead to success. She saw that the ever-more-complicated strategies she was pursuing were not bringing in better results. In fact, her results were getting worse.

Euphoria - then Despair

Going from euphoria to despair, often in the same month and sometimes in the same week, was exhausting. Finally, after one too many sleepless nights pacing the floor, sick with worry, she decided enough was enough.

Yet again, her stocks were plummeting, and her dreams of financial freedom were disappearing. She knew that she couldn't go on like that. Something had to change. She had to find a better way. And she did. It's called the:

The ITM Strategy

When she stepped back and looked at things from a different perspective, she realized that the solution had been staring her in the face all the time. It was simple and elegant - and it meant no more sleepless nights and endless hours of research.

In her first book **In The Money: Bull Market Strategy,** she shares with you the ITM Strategy that she uses to beat the market. It's easy and takes less than 10 minutes a week. She gives a simple set of rules that anyone, beginner or seasoned trader, can follow and be sure to beat the market and build their wealth.

Her second book was an overseas version of **In The Money: Bull Market Strategy** for people wanting to trade the U.S. market but living outside the U.S.

The third book in the series, **In The Money: Bear Market Strategy,** was written in response to the many readers asking for a book on how to handle a bear market. It shows exactly how and what to trade when the stock market has entered bear territory.

Reader requests and queries also prompted the fourth book, **Compare Option Strategies**. Part textbook and part workbook, it guides the reader through choosing options and trading strategies.

Annoyed by misleading advice by financial 'experts' claiming that the 'buy-and-hold' strategy produced the best returns, she wrote her fifth book **Timing The Market** which debunks the theory that 'time in the market' was the best investment strategy. It shows a simple way to time the market that increases your returns by 50%.

Options Trading for Beginners, her sixth book, was an easy introduction to options and how to trade them.

You don't have to make the same mistakes

In her books, Heather shares with you her rocky journey from failure to financial freedom. Her many errors and losses are not glossed over. Instead, she openly shares them so that you don't have to make the same mistakes.

She looks on her losses as 'tuition fees' for the lessons learned, and she has paid a LOT of tuition fees over the years. You will probably have a laugh over some of the things she has done. She can laugh now, but at the time she wasn't laughing as she watched her dreams of financial freedom disappearing yet again.

Today, she has not worked in a job for almost twenty years, and has the financial freedom she always sought. Writing, travelling, learning – it's a life she loves.

You'll Never Trade Alone

Heather writes a free weekly blog on the stock market and ITM strategy. She analyzes the charts, alerts readers if actions need to be taken and answers readers' questions. Here's the link:

HeatherCullen.com / Blog

(Or google 'Heather Cullen Blog'.)

Heather Cullen

HeatherCullen.com

Trade the tide,
not the waves

Books by Heather Cullen

In The Money Series

In The Money: Bull Market Strategy

In The Money: Overseas Edition

In The Money: Bear Market Strategy

Compare Option Strategies

One Hour Expert Series

Timing The Market

Options Trading for Beginners

Reading Stock Charts

Contact Heather Cullen

Hi! I love to hear from readers and read every email I get. I have a free weekly blog on the market and strategies, so if you have any questions or comments, please contact me there and I will happily respond. Here's the link.

HeatherCullen.com / Blog

Reviews

If you liked the **Reading Stock Charts,** I would really appreciate a review on Amazon. To find me quickly just google *'Heather Cullen Amazon Reading Stock Charts'* and then scroll down to reviews.

"Another lesson I learned early is that there is nothing new in Wall Street. There can't be because speculation is as old as the hills. Whatever happens in the stock market today has happened before and will happen again."

Jesse Livermore

(The original Wolf of Wall St)

Reminiscences of a Stock Operator

Printed in Dunstable, United Kingdom